101 More Uses for a
Dead Cat

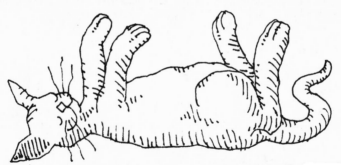

by Simon Bond

Clarkson N. Potter, Inc./Publishers NEW Y
DISTRIBUTED BY CROWN PUBLISHERS, IN

Published by Clarkson N. Potter, Inc.,
One Park Avenue, New York, New York 10016

Manufactured in the United States of America

Library of Congress Cataloging in Publication Data
Bond, Simon.
    101 more uses for a dead cat.
    Sequel to: 101 uses for a dead cat.
    Includes index.
    1. Cats—Caricatures and cartoons.   2. American
wit and humor, Pictorial.   I. Title.   II. Title:
One hundred and one more uses for a dead cat.
NC1429.B663A4   1982a   741.5 973   82-6424
ISBN: 0-517-547465   AACR2

10   9   8   7   6   5   4   3   2   1

First Edition

4

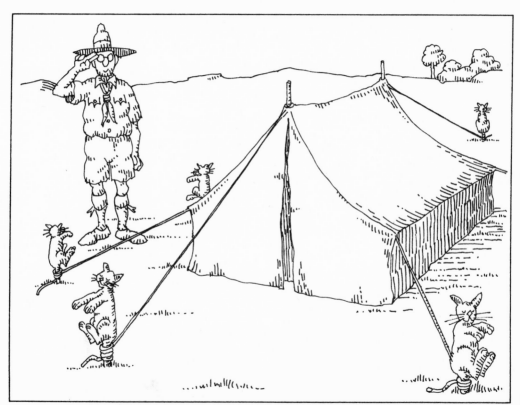

5

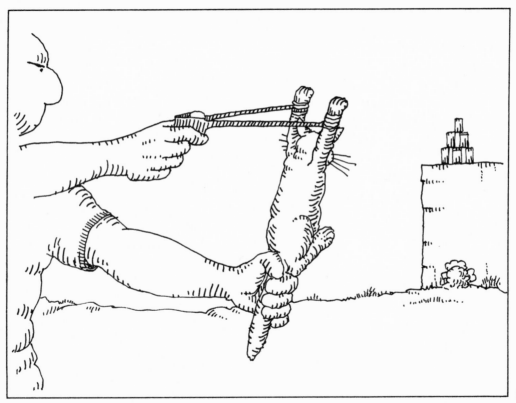

9

13

17

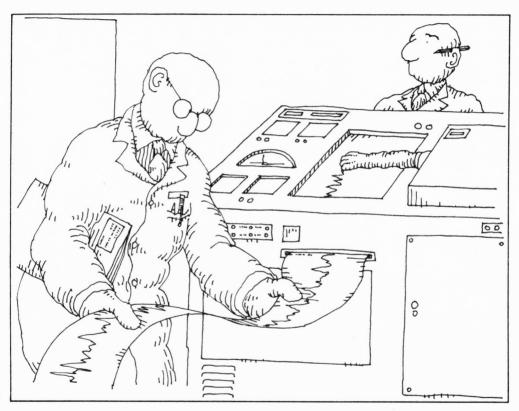

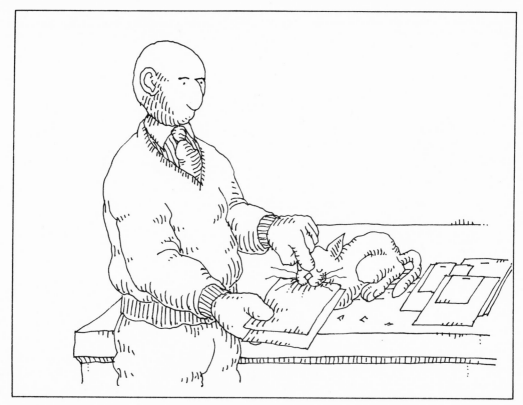

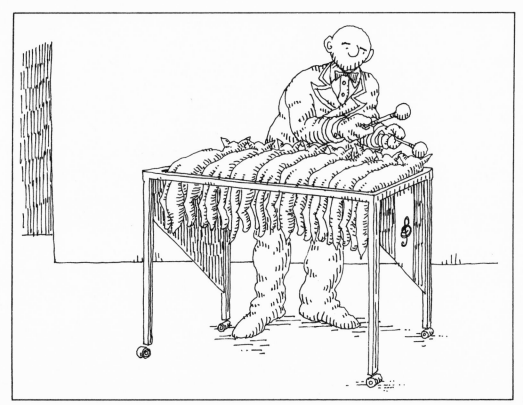

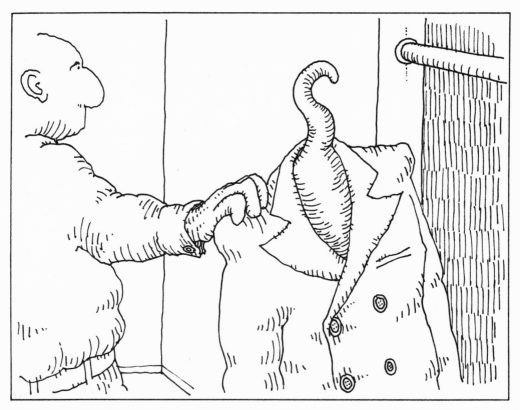

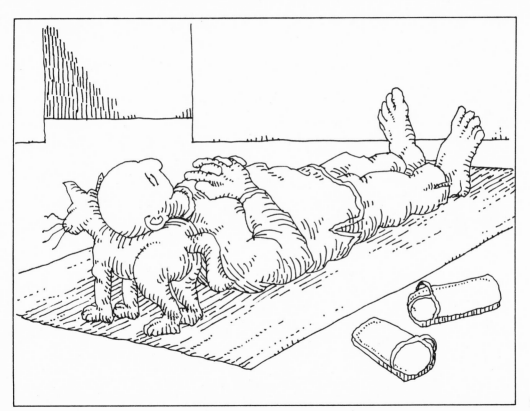

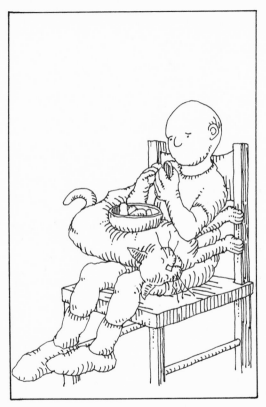

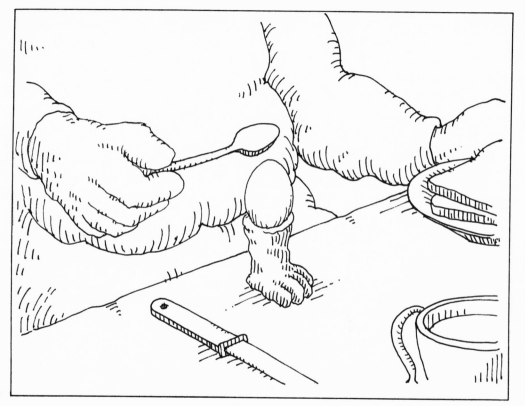

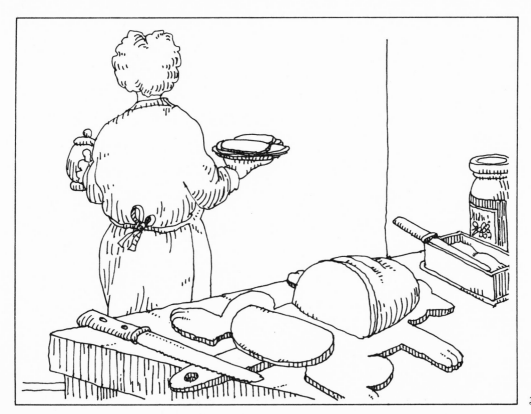

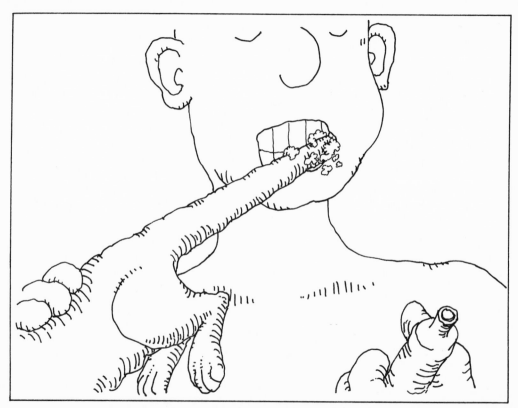

41

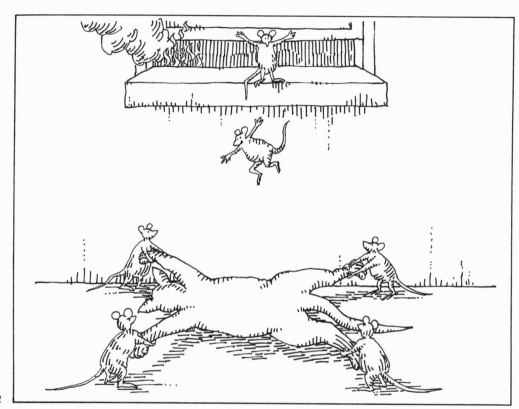

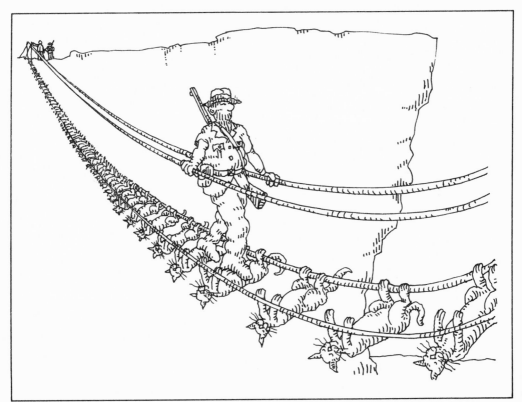

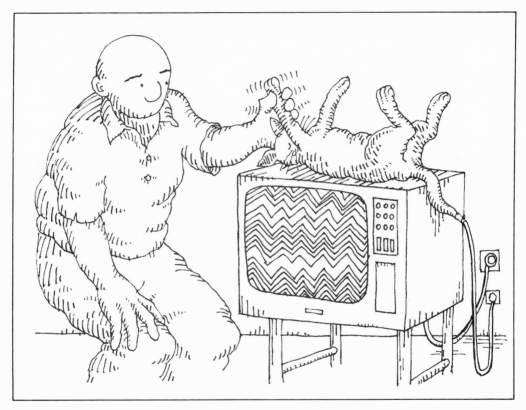

51

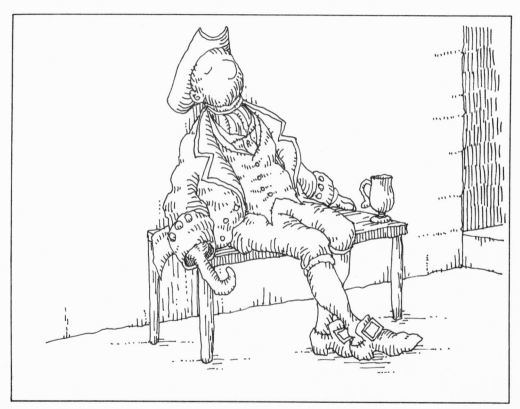

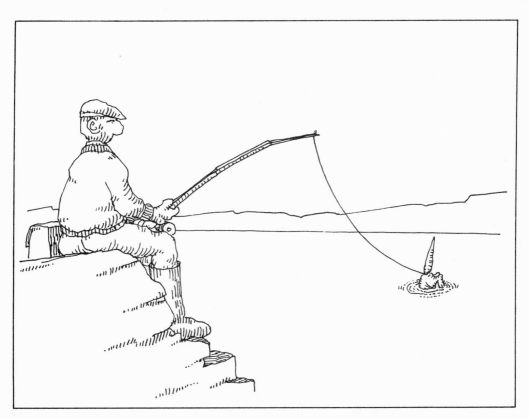

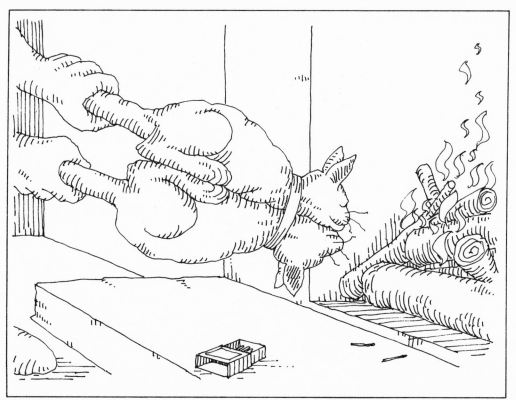

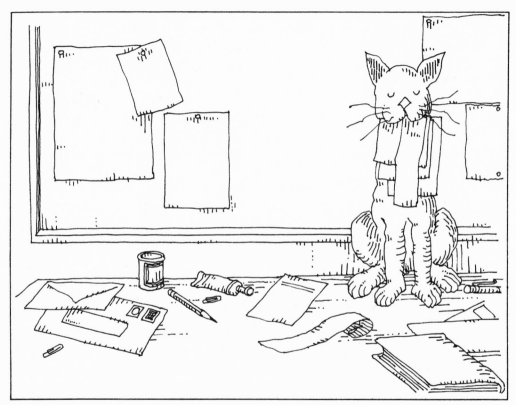

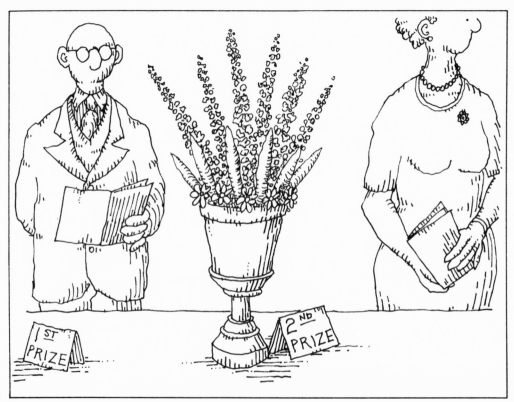

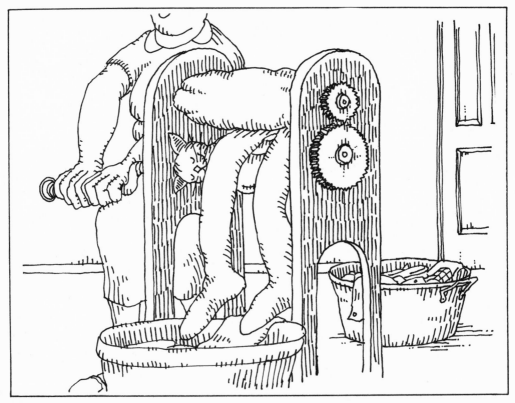

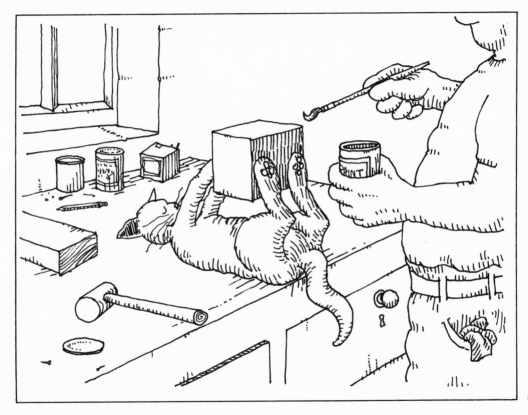

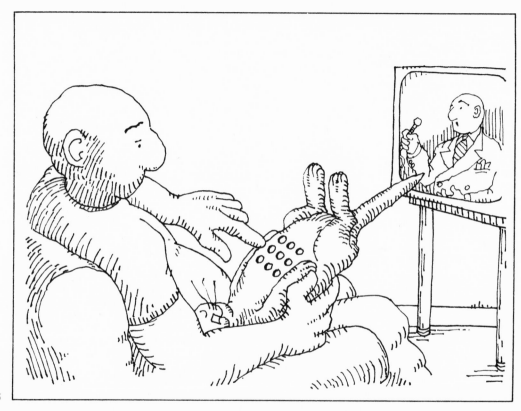

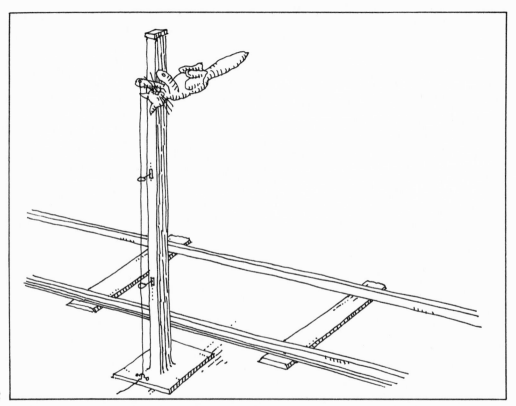

Index of Uses